Prentice Hall

WRITING and GRAMMAR

Communication in Action

Gold Level

Topic Bank for Heterogeneous Classes

ISBN 0-13-043908-8

1 2 3 4 5 6 7 8 9 10   04 03 02 01 00

Contents

Note: This booklet contains topic ideas to extend the Topic Bank that appears in Chapters 4–15 of the student book.

Introduction

Description

This *Topic Bank for Heterogeneous Classes* is designed to be used with Part 1 of *Prentice Hall Writing and Grammar: Communication in Action*. It supports the Topic Bank found in Chapters 4–15. For each chapter, there are twelve to fifteen writing prompts. These pages are blackline masters, which you may copy and distribute to students.

The number and variety of writing assignments address the needs, abilities, and interests of students in your classes. The first group of writing ideas in each Topic Bank is suitable for your average students. Those labeled "Less Challenging" are simpler concepts requiring less effort; these are more suitable for your less able students. Those labeled "More Challenging" are usually more sophisticated topics, requiring more in-depth thinking; these are suitable for your more advanced learners. It is often effective to allow students to work on a topic of their own choosing, however, regardless of the labels. The Cooperative Activities will give your students an opportunity to work together in a group or with a partner.

Suggestions for Use

- Instruct students in developing a type of writing, using the strategies in the writing chapters in *Writing and Grammar: Communication in Action*. If students are unable to come up with an appropriate topic for their writing, give them the Topic Bank prompts from which to choose.
- Give students a writing prompt from the Topic Bank first and then refer them to the corresponding chapter in *Writing and Grammar: Communication in Action*.
- Allow students to choose the assignment they wish to complete.
- Select the assignments you feel are appropriate for each individual.

Assessing Students' Work

Refer students to the corresponding chapter in *Writing and Grammar: Communication in Action*, where they will find guidelines and strategies for each type of writing and a rubric for self-assessment. You may wish to use the rubric in scoring students' work. You will also find scoring models in *Writing Assessment and Portfolio Management* in the Teaching Resources.

Topic Bank for Chapter 4

Narration: Autobiographical Writing

1. No matter how carefully an event or project is planned, something may still go wrong. Write an autobiographical incident about a significant event in your life that turned out quite different from what you had expected, such as when you made a fool of yourself in front of someone you wanted to impress.

2. Think about a time when you visited another country very different from yours, or met someone who is from a distant country. Write a personal essay about your experience. What new customs did you learn from your trip or from the person you met? How has your exposure to a different country, or to someone from a different country, changed your perspective on the United States?

3. Occasionally, a person is asked to perform a rather disagreeable task, which he or she would rather avoid. Have you ever been asked to perform a task you really didn't want to do? Perhaps you had to give someone some bad news, clean out a basement, or attend a dull event. Write a personal essay about an occasion when you performed an unpleasant task. Why did you find the task unpleasant and how did you cope with it?

4. While most people see large wild animals in zoo exhibits or on television programs, we all have had experiences with smaller wild animals such as birds, squirrels, or raccoons. What experiences have you had involving an animal in the wild? Write an autobiographical account of your experience.

Less Challenging

5. The excitement and tension surrounding sports events—such as baseball, basketball, and football games—make them great topics for narratives. Think about an exciting experience you've had with baseball or any other sport—either as a player or as a spectator. Write an autobiographical essay in which you re-create your experience. Include a detailed description of the event as well as your experience.

6. When fans approach celebrities in public, some celebrities stop to sign autographs while others flee to a private location. Have you ever met a celebrity? Write an autobiographical account of the encounter. Did the person look the same in person as he or she does on screen or in magazine photographs? Were you able to ask him or her any questions?

7. We learn about nature not only in the classroom, but also through everyday experiences. Write a personal essay about a time when you learned something interesting and exciting about nature, and show how this has influenced your way of thinking. What was it that you learned about nature and how did you learn it? Explain how your appreciation of nature has changed.

More Challenging

8. Choose a novel, short story, essay, poem, or play that you particularly like or with which you identify. Write a personal essay in which you describe a real-life incident similar to one in the literary work. Include an explanation of how your reading changed your mind about an issue, or how it helped you solve a problem.

9. Older people tend to be very wise. A lifetime of valuable experiences, and the time they have had to reflect on them, are reasons for their wisdom. Is there an older person in your life who has shared some of his or her wisdom by offering good advice? Write a personal essay describing a time you received valuable advice from an older person. Include an explanation of how the advice has affected your life.

10. By working together, two people are often able to complete a task more quickly while learning from each other. Think of a time when you worked with someone else—either an adult or someone your own age. What task was involved and what new skills or information did you learn? Write a personal essay about the experience.

11. Choose your first name, your last name, or both, and see what you can find out about their origins. If your name can't be traced, speculate about where it may have come from. Is your name unusual or difficult to pronounce? What would you have named yourself? How do you feel when you hear your name or see it in print? Write a reflective essay in which you explore your name's origins, discuss your feelings about it, and consider the impact your name has had on the development of your personality.

Cooperative Activity

12. Work with a group to write a collection of autobiographical essays. As a group, decide on a theme for the collection, such as significant family events, happy childhood memories, or fun school activities. Each person should write an autobiographical sketch relating to the chosen theme. Exchange papers with someone in the group and suggest revisions for improvement. Compile all the essays into a booklet. Include photographs or drawings to accompany each essay.

Topic Bank for Chapter 5

Narration: Short Story

1. Believe it or not, you can develop a great story based on a few details of a news event. Watch the evening news and leaf through a few newspapers. You may consider the top events of the day or look beyond them to the sports, entertainment, and society news. Select an event in the news that captures your interest and write a short story about it. Use your imagination to fill in the details of one of the stories, or create a new story on a related issue.

2. Many people think of caves as quiet or even silent places. In fact, caves can be a source of a variety of interesting sounds, such as water dripping on limestone, echoes of voices, or the flapping of bats' wings. Write a short story involving characters exploring a cave. Focus on describing the different sounds in the cave to help create a mood of suspense.

3. People's talents lie in many different areas—athletics, drawing or graphic design, scientific inquiry, crafts, music or some other performing art, and dozens of others. Write a short story in which you start by developing the character. Create a main character who is exceptionally good at something. Take your readers into the life of this character by telling the story of how the character uses his or her talents to resolve a conflict.

4. Whether it's an attic, a thick branch in a maple tree, a certain table at the pizza parlor, or a cozy armchair by a window, the world is filled with special places. Develop a character for a short story by selecting a place that is special to your character in some way. Is it a room in a house, a strip of sandy beach, or an entire city? Or, is it an imaginary place that the character always *wanted* to visit? Consider what makes this place special to him or her. Write a short story in which you create a vivid picture of this special place and capture what it means to the character.

Less Challenging

5. Dramatic landscapes and other aspects of the natural world have inspired countless short stories. Find a photograph that shows a landscape (or some other part of nature, such as a majestic tree or storm clouds) that you find inspiring. Then, write a short story that takes place in this landscape. Introduce your characters and develop the plot and conflict.

6. Holidays and other celebrations around the world often feature colorful lights and costumes, parades, fairs, fireworks, music, or dancing. Choose a celebration in which you have participated and write a short story describing the excitement of this event. Use descriptive adjectives to suggest the mood of celebration.

7. Most short stories revolve around a central event. Think about an actual event that you have witnessed, read about, or experienced, or create one that's memorable. Write a short story revolving around that event. Introduce and develop a conflict that the characters face. Show how this problem is resolved.

More Challenging

8. Stories of action, adventure, and suspense often take place in unusual locations, such as a jungle, a tropical island, or a foreign city. Choose an exotic setting and write a suspenseful or action-packed short story involving a conflict between at least two characters. Be sure to show how the setting affects the characters and the action of the drama.

9. Sequels to popular stories or movies are usually quite successful. Once audiences get attached to particular characters, they want to learn more about them. Choose your favorite short story from your literature anthology. Using the same character, setting, conflict, and theme, write a *prequel* (a short story that depicts what happens before the events of the first short story) or a *sequel* (what happens after the short story ends).

10. When you travel with someone, you often get to know that person in ways you wouldn't otherwise. Write a humorous short story about two people traveling together. Explain who the characters are and where they are going. Focus on the interaction between the characters. What conflicts do these characters face?

11. The nomadic lifestyle of the Plains Indians was built around hunting bison. When the bison disappeared from the Great Plains, however, these Native Americans' way of life disappeared also. Think about the effect—either positive or negative—of major changes in people's lives. Write a short story about the effects of change. Focus your short story either on changes faced by a specific group of people or on the effects of change in general.

Cooperative Activity

12. Working with a group, create a short novel in which short stories serve as chapters. The group should decide on the novel's plot, setting, characters, conflict, and conflict resolution. Based on the plan for the book, each person should choose a chapter to write; or, you may randomly select who writes which chapter. As a group, read the short stories aloud to make sure the novel reads smoothly. Make revisions if necessary. Compile the chapters into a booklet and create a title and a cover for your novel.

Topic Bank for Chapter 6

Description

1. Sunsets have long been a source of inspiration for writers and artists. Write a description of a beautiful sunset that you've witnessed, or describe a sunset that you have seen on television or in a photo. Use precise words to capture the vivid colors of the sunset, the effect of the sunset on the landscape, and the feelings or emotions the sunset evoked.

2. Survival stories fascinate and inspire people because they arouse fear, awe, and respect. Find a survivor in your family or your community, such as a neighbor who lived through an earthquake or a tornado. Brainstorm for a list of questions to obtain facts and specific details of the experience. Then, interview the survivor. Based on the information you get, write a description of the incident that emphasizes the qualities of the person that made survival possible.

3. The informal definition of a *character* is "a peculiar or eccentric person." Choose the most unconventional person you know and write a descriptive portrait of him or her. Include distinct physical features and mannerisms, unique personal style of dress, and characteristic ways of thinking and talking. Try to bring this unusual person to life on the page, helping your readers to understand why he or she is a *character*.

4. Unlike traditional news stories that report mainly on current events, newspaper and magazine profiles often focus on fascinating people who have unconventional hobbies or interesting professions. Choose someone in your community whom you would like to know more about and whose experiences are apt to be very different from yours. You might consider a private detective, a chimney sweep, a radio disc jockey, or a rock climber. Gather information by observing and interviewing the subject, by talking to people who know her or him, and by doing library research. Then, immortalize your subject in a profile that is both factual and entertaining.

Less Challenging

5. When we return to a place we visited earlier in our lives, it often turns out to be different from how we remembered it. Think of a place you returned to after being away from it for an extended period of time—your elementary school, a vacation site, a neighborhood where you once lived, or a relative's home, for example. Write a remembrance in which you describe your memories of this place; compare them to what you discovered when you returned there. In your description, use vivid details, images, and figurative language.

6. Think of people you know very well. Then, try to recall your first encounter with each one. Decide which of these encounters is most memorable. Write a remembrance of this first encounter. Try to capture what made this first meeting so memorable.

7. Imagine that you work for the special effects department of a movie studio in Hollywood. Your assignment is to describe a battle between two monsters for a new movie that's currently in production. Use your imagination to create the two monsters and to come up with the details of their battle. How big are the monsters and what color are they? What unusual physical features and personality traits cause them to be monsters? Use the details you've come up with to write your description. Use vivid action verbs to describe precisely the actions that take place in the fight itself.

More Challenging

8. Drama has entertained human beings from earliest times; it is the genre that most directly engages its audience. Audiences flock to professional and amateur productions, children love "playacting," and students enjoy writing and performing skits. What is it about drama that has such appeal? Write a description of a play. In your description, explain the characteristics of a play and indicate how they contribute to drama's strong appeal.

9. Imagine that you are a famous person from another century. If you had been composer Ludwig von Beethoven, emperor Montezuma, explorer Vasco Núñez de Balboa, outlaw Jesse James, or reformer Harriet Tubman, what possession would you have valued the most? Write a description of this object from the perspective of its owner, reminiscing about its place in your life.

10. Select a natural image from one of your favorite poems. Try to find a line, or a group of lines, that enables you to see, feel, hear, smell, and almost taste some sensation, experience, or scene. Using the image as a starting point, write a description that develops the word picture. As you describe this aspect of nature, try to include appropriate emotions and ideas that will bring the image to life.

11. Outstanding athletes like Michael Jordan, Martina Navratilova, or Wayne Gretzky are able to do things that other people can only dream about. Even those who witness the performance of athletes like these can't always believe their eyes. Such people are called "naturals" for the apparent ease with which they've mastered their skills. Write a description of a natural, using specific details and examples of someone who is a natural in his or her sport.

Cooperative Activity

12. When Michael Jordan and other professional basketball stars joined forces on the 1992 U.S. Olympic team, their all-star quality earned them the nickname "the Dream Team." As a group, choose a team sport you all enjoy. Compile a list of all-star athletes from that sport. Have each group member choose a different listed athlete and write a description of that player in action. In each description, capture the qualities that make the player an all-star. Then, work together to assemble the descriptions into an all-star roster. You may want to find photographs to accompany the descriptions.

Topic Bank for Chapter 7

Persuasion: Persuasive Essay

1. The only opportunity many people have to see exotic or rare animals is in a zoo or other place where the animals are held in captivity. Write a position paper about whether keeping animals in captivity is a good idea. Be sure to clearly state your position and to support it with reasons and facts.

2. Many professional athletes are paid enormous amounts of money to play their sport. In addition, many receive large sums to endorse various products—athletic shoes, tennis racquets, soft drinks, and so on. Some people think that professional athletes are overpaid, while others think they receive a fair wage. Write a persuasive speech in which you express your opinion. Use facts and examples to support the validity of your opinion.

3. Your school system is considering adding community service to the requirements for high school graduation. Many parents, teachers, and students object, claiming that volunteer programs would take time away from studying, sports, extracurricular activities, and part-time jobs. Take a stand on volunteering and write a letter to the editor of your school newspaper that will persuade readers to see this issue as you do.

4. Many people believe that human emotion can alter the way history is reported, sometimes making it less than factual. Objective information is important for historians searching for the causes of events. Yet, historians also find subjective sources, such as firsthand accounts from people involved in historical events, to be valuable in determining what life was like at a given time. Write a position paper in which you state your opinion about the need for objectivity, or being neutral, in reporting historical events.

Less Challenging

5. Many schools provide very expensive equipment, such as athletic shoes, to student athletes. Some people believe that school money could be better spent for purely academic purposes, whereas others think that athletics are an important part of the educational experience. Write a persuasive essay to express your position on this issue. Support your stance with relevant facts and, if possible, personal experience.

6. As a roller skater who has recently converted to in-line skates, you are excited that you will be able to spend more time skating outdoors. Unfortunately, the jogging and walking track where you had hoped to skate has just been declared off-limits to in-line skaters. Write a letter to the editor of your local newspaper protesting this new ruling. In addition to defining the problem and identifying and evaluating possible solutions, be sure to respond to the reasons for barring skaters. Alternatively, write the same letter from the point of view of a jogger or walker.

7. Your club or team is planning a fund-raising event for charity. While some members support the traditional bake sale or car wash, others would like to try something new, such as an auction or an ethnic festival. Write a letter to the editor of the school newspaper in which you take a stand on this debate. Choose a fund-raising method that you believe would be most enjoyable and most profitable. Use logical reasoning and specific examples to persuade your fellow students to resolve the issue your way.

8. Miguel de Cervantes poses an interesting question in this quotation from *Don Quixote*, "Can we ever have too much of a good thing?" Think of situations from real life or literature that relate to the question. Then, write a persuasive essay in which you try to convince others to accept your answer. Use examples from your life to support your argument.

More Challenging

9. The reduction of natural habitats is one of the primary reasons animals are becoming endangered. Yet, humans need to develop new lands in order to accommodate growing populations. What do you think is the proper balance between preserving natural wildlife habitats and supporting development for human expansion? Write a persuasive essay in which you present your views on this issue.

10. Getting a new sport admitted into the Olympic Games takes a combination of political clout and dedication. Finding a sponsor to back the sport and its participants and holding enough competitions to prove the popularity of the sport are two steps involved in the process. Arousing public interest and support, however, is one of the most important ways to lobby for a new sport. Write an editorial for a sports magazine in which you provide logical arguments for why snowboarding, skateboarding, windsurfing, or the sport of your choice should be part of the Winter or Summer Games.

11. "One never knows when one might be indebted to even the lowliest of beggars." This quotation from Yoshiko Uchida's "Of Dry Goods and Black Bow Ties" suggests that everyone should be treated with respect. Do you agree or disagree with the quotation? Write an essay to support your opinion of the need to treat everyone with respect. Use examples to support your opinion.

Cooperative Activity

12. Work with a partner to present both sides of a historical conflict. You might, for example, write a persuasive essay about the causes of the American Revolution, attempting to convince your reader to agree with your point of view. Choose a historical event that is familiar to both of you. Each person should write an essay from a different point of view. Place the two essays on a poster board with illustrations to represent both arguments.

Topic Bank for Chapter 8

Persuasion: Advertisement

1. Imagine that you and your family have some experience with river rafting. What would help you decide whether or not to try a weekend rafting trip with a camping outfit? Would you want to know about your guide? Your food and accommodation? Your horse? Write a magazine advertisement for a weekend whitewater trip in the mountains. Use concrete details to describe the experiences people have had on the trip. Be specific about comforts provided, hours spent rafting, experience of the guides, and price of the trip.

2. Have you thought about having a place for teenagers to gather and socialize in your community? Do you know what adults think about the idea? Interview some of your friends and some adults to understand about the pros and cons. Then, write a public-service advertisement for your local cable access station in which you try to get politicians in your community to support the creation of a teen center. Use logical and emotional arguments to convince them that everyone would benefit from such a center. In practical terms, explain step by step the ways the center could be funded.

3. Imagine that there is a new bakery near the high school and the owners are eager for publicity among teenagers who walk by the shop. Create a poster campaign advertising the bakery to students. Start with photographs of homemade muffins and pastries, as well as pictures of the cozy tables and friendly counter staff inside the bakery. Write an advertisement that will appeal to teenagers and coax them to stop in the bakery for snacks.

4. Have you ever taken a course outside of school? Have you studied watercolor painting? Karate? Carpentry? Write a magazine advertisement for a course, or set of courses, with which you are familiar. Use a picture or photograph to show the students engaged in the activity. Relate the content of the course to teenagers' goals. Use sensory language to describe the enjoyable experiences offered by the course.

Less Challenging

5. Advertising a movie involves a delicate balancing act. You want to grab the viewers' interest, but without giving away too much of the plot. Suppose you are promoting a new film. Write a newspaper advertisement convincing people to see it. Choose an exciting visual image to represent the film, and write a line or two that hints at the major conflict in the story. Describe the characters and praise the acting. Use words that appeal to the reader's senses to re-create the sights, sounds, and emotions in the film.

6. Suppose you want to run a small business this summer and you need investors to help you finance the business. Write an advertisement for your local newspaper in which you attempt to interest local financiers in your idea. First, describe the business as you see it in the future. Then, explain what you require to get the business there. Be specific about your skills and enthusiasm, and specify the financial return you expect to give investors at the end of the summer.

7. Have you been active in a volunteer organization? Has the organization been short of workers? Create a cable television advertisement to convince other students to participate in your volunteer group.

Find an appealing photograph of the group activity. Using descriptive and encouraging language, make your viewers part of that picture. Be sure to relate your viewers' goals to the activity.

More Challenging

8. Are you strongly attached to a particular brand of shoes, jackets, or jeans? Could you convince a potential buyer of your opinion? Create a visual of your clothing item, either a photograph or an illustration. Then, write a magazine advertisement using the brand name, the visual, and a convincing verbal argument. Be as specific and engaging as you can about what this item of clothing does for you.

9. What is the most useful piece of furniture in your home? Could you sell other pieces like it? Write a television advertisement for this piece of furniture. Create a storyboard—panels of consecutive visuals and text that represent the script for the advertisement. Use a dialogue or a monologue to describe the function, comfort, and beauty of the piece.

10. Trains that run above the ground may soon be available in your area. Find out more about how these trains are scheduled and how it feels to ride in them. Then, write a magazine advertisement for an above-ground train, convincing the public that it will be convenient, safe, and efficient for riders. Emphasize its speed, comfort, cleanliness, and safety. Be specific about price, features, and availability.

11. Have you ever written to a member of the Senate or House of Representatives? Multiple letters on one topic can be very effective in determining votes on particular bills. Write an imaginary bill that will provide low-income housing to more families around the nation. Write a public-service announcement encouraging the public to contact their Senator or Representative in support of the bill.

Cooperative Activity

12. Have you ever attended and enjoyed a concert performed by a local band? Imagine that they have asked you to promote their next performance. With a partner, write a promotion for a musical group that you both like. Each person should research a different topic for the advertisement. Interview the band to find out more about their background in music, the instruments they use, and the message they are trying to convey. Prepare a television advertisement that includes quotes from the band, recordings, photographs, and text that promotes the concert. Specify the instruments used and describe the style and themes of two or three songs. Use sensory language to describe what their concerts are like.

Topic Bank for Chapter 9

Exposition: Comparison-and-Contrast Essay

1. Although various presidents of the United States have faced similar issues over the years, most have handled the situations differently. Select two American presidents and compare and contrast their approach to certain issues, such as environmental protection, foreign policy, education, and health care. In your essay, explore the similarities and differences between the presidents' policies.

2. Most people share the opinion that flowers are all beautiful yet very different from each other. Choose two different types of flowers. Think about how these flowers are similar and how they are different. Consider elements such as size, shape, color, texture, smell, and required growing conditions. Write an essay comparing and contrasting the two flowers.

3. As the consumer reporter for your school newspaper, you often evaluate products that interest teenagers. For this month's column you will compare two products, such as two makes of sneakers or two brands of jeans. Decide on the features you will consider in judging the two products, such as design, cost, fit, and durability. Write a newspaper article in which you recommend one of the products as superior to the other.

4. Articles of sports equipment—ranging from tennis sneakers and softballs to field hockey sticks and tumbling mats—are usually designed with performance, durability, and safety in mind. Some pieces of equipment are better than others, however, and nearly every model has both positive and negative characteristics. Choose two brands of a piece of sports equipment you use frequently. Write an essay in which you compare and contrast the superior and inferior qualities of the two brands.

Less Challenging

5. When we decide what foods to buy, we usually do a quick comparison and contrast in our heads. Think about a food product you enjoy—perhaps crackers, juice, or pizza. Then, write an essay in which you compare and contrast two different brands of the same product. Include comparisons of the items' taste, freshness, and nutritional value.

6. Helicopters and airplanes are the two most common types of air transport. Although they look very different, both serve many of the same purposes. Think about how helicopters and airplanes are used. In what ways are they similar and how are they different? Compare and contrast these two types of transport in a brief essay.

7. You have been selected to serve on the committee that will choose your new school mascot. Select two mascots that you think would effectively represent the spirit of your community and school. The mascots should not be offensive or insulting to anyone. Write an essay comparing and contrasting your choices.

8. Student A prefers to walk to school. She can leave when she is ready without having to worry about the bus schedule, and she appreciates the physical fitness benefits she gets from walking. Student B prefers the comfort of taking the bus. He likes to avoid inclement weather as much as possible, and he appreciates the opportunity to

socialize with his friends. These two students want you to decide which method is better. Write an essay comparing and contrasting these two methods of traveling to school.

More Challenging

9. The United States is an enormous country that covers more than 3.5 million square miles. Moreover, the nation's landmass contains a remarkable variety of habitats and climates, ranging from the frigid wilderness of northern Alaska to the desert wilderness of the Southwest. Find out more about the extreme climates of these American wilderness regions. Then, write an essay in which you compare and contrast two or more of these regions.

10. Baseball in the mid-1800's had many similarities to the way baseball is played today. Even so, there have been many rule changes in the game since that time. For example, in the early days, the winner was decided by the first team to reach 21 runs. Consider what other differences there are between how we play the game today and how the game was played in the past. Write a comparison-and-contrast essay of the sport in the two eras.

11. In order to increase students' understanding of history and civilization as a series of repeating cycles, the Social Studies Department at your school has decided to publish a book. You have been asked to contribute an article. Choose two leaders, such as Alexander the Great and Napoleon; two groups of people, such as the Aztecs and the Cherokees; or two events, such as the Boston Tea Party and the Boxer Rebellion. After doing library research, write a comparison-and-contrast essay in which you analyze the similarities and differences between the people or events. Consider how these people or events support the notion that history repeats itself.

12. Think of fictional characters from literature, television, or movies with which you are familiar. Choose two characters from different works who find themselves in similar situations. Compare and contrast how they handle the situation. Conclude your essay with your judgment about which character acted more wisely.

Cooperative Activity

13. You may take for granted how money looks and feels. Yet, if you travel to another country, you will handle a variety of unusual bills and coins. You can learn something about a culture's values from the design of its currency. For instance, national heroes, landmarks, and other political symbols often appear on a nation's money. With a group of classmates, make a list of nations whose currencies you'd like to explore. Then, have each group member research the currency of one country and write a brief essay that compares and contrasts that nation's currency with American money. As a group, assemble the essays into a booklet called *Currencies of the World*. If possible, obtain pictures or actual samples of the currencies to incorporate into your booklet.

Topic Bank for Chapter 10

Exposition: Cause-and-Effect Essay

1. Use the library to research various aspects of a particular marine-life food chain. In descending order, from larger fish to smaller fish, describe in an essay the cause-and-effect relationships involved in the chain. Specify the habits of the larger fish and the defensive mechanisms of the smaller fish to fully describe the dynamic.

2. Do you know any techniques used in training a large animal, such as a horse or an elephant? By reading about this subject and interviewing experts, gather information about how trainers successfully control these animals. Write an essay explaining how good techniques elicit desired behavior in the animal and how improper training can have the opposite effect. Include positive and negative reinforcement techniques.

3. Are you familiar with a particular sport, such as football or volleyball? Do you understand how strategy can help your team get points in the game? Interview experts and read training manuals to gather more information about strategies for your chosen sport. Then, write an essay explaining the strategies, the causes and effects involved, and how players and coaches work to win games.

4. Do you understand what causes a major storm, such as a tornado or hurricane? Choose a type of storm that could occur in your region of the country and research the causes and effects of those storms. Then, identify one particular storm that occurred in your region and learn about its specific causes and effects. Write an essay, first explaining the meteorological basis for the type of storm, then describing the progression of the specific storm.

Less Challenging

5. Have you ever had a really bad cold? Do you know what caused your cold and what controlled its symptoms? Do some library research about the cold virus. Then, write an essay explaining step by step what factors can contribute to a cold and what treatments can control its symptoms. Explain how to avoid a cold and, if you get one, how to make it easier to tolerate.

6. Have you thought about how exercise affects certain muscles in your body? Choose a muscle group, such as biceps or quadriceps, and find out how they change with certain types of exercise. After doing some research, make diagrams showing the muscle before and after specific periods of time doing an exercise. Then, write an essay explaining the process in chronological order.

7. Have you ever had an argument with a friend and then tried to piece together how it developed? Reconstruct a real or imagined argument; take notes about what happened and what each party said, in sequence. Then, write an essay objectively explaining the causes and effects of each incident and/or statement that occurred. Try to see where one or both of you could have said or done something to resolve the argument sooner.

8. Imagine that you fish for a living. You don't want to waste fuel or subject your boat to unnecessary wear and tear by fishing when the fish don't run or when the weather is bad. Do some research about how fish behave in a particular place. What causes the fish to behave this way? How does this affect your plans? Then, make a plan for outfitting your boat and choose times of day and seasons when you will fish most actively. Write an essay summarizing your plan.

More Challenging

9. Have you ever wondered about the causes and effects of a particular war such as World War I? Research the chronology of that war and determine causes and effects. Using index cards, logically group these causes and effects in an ordered narrative. Then, write an essay explaining those causes and effects. For extra credit, consider factors that could have avoided the war.

10. Have you thought about the factors that affect economic recession? Do some library research about recent recessions. Also, interview one or two experts about the significant causes and effects of those recessions. Write an essay in which you incorporate what you learn. Make suggestions for avoiding recession in the future.

11. Air pollution is caused by auto emissions, factory emissions, and various types of smoke from wood stoves, fireplaces, and bonfires. Using data from environmental groups over the past ten years, find out which factor has had the most detrimental effect on air quality in your area. Write an essay in which you explain how this factor affects air quality.

Cooperative Activity

12. Young children respond to direction and discipline in various ways. Some ways of guiding children are more effective than others. Get permission to go with a partner to observe several different pre-school classrooms; visit each for a few hours. One person should record verbal interactions between teacher and students about expected behavior; the other person should record the actual behavior of the students in response to direction. Write individual essays and then get together to decide which methods were most effective. Combine the two essays into one essay describing the cause-and-effect processes you observed in the classroom and giving advice to the teachers.

Topic Bank for Chapter 11

Exposition: Problem-and-Solution Essay

1. Each year, your grade celebrates the end of the school year with an awards banquet. As chairperson of the festivities, you must work with a committee to decide where the celebration should be held. This year, there is conflict about which venue would be best. Write a memo to the faculty sponsor explaining the different sides of the problem. Include a discussion of the solutions under consideration and evaluate each one. Conclude your memo with a recommendation about which course of action is the most viable one.

2. You work at a company as a troubleshooter. Whenever a problem arises, it is your responsibility to analyze the situation and figure out how to fix it in the most cost-effective and efficient manner. Imagine a problem that surfaces in your company. Write a report that first explains the exact nature of the problem. Then detail, step by step, how you intend to solve the problem. Explain why your solution is better than other solutions that might also be presented.

3. Although you were once a dedicated fan of a television situation comedy about teenagers, you have grown bored with the program. You think that with a little work, however, it can be improved. Write a letter to the producer and director analyzing why the program is no longer as good as it was. Suggest some ways it might be improved.

4. When you ask "what if . . ." questions, you are thinking about creative solutions to a problematic situation in which the steps toward reaching the goal are not immediately apparent. Choose one of the "what if" problems listed below and try to view it from as many different angles as possible—think beyond the commonplace and the ingrained. Write an essay in which you offer as many resourceful solutions as you can, giving examples from personal experience to lend credence to your ideas. What would happen if . . .

- sleep were unnecessary?
- people were satisfied with things as they are?
- we had another set of eyes in the back of our heads?

Less Challenging

5. Is there a problem within one of your school's student organizations that you could investigate? A disagreement about authority? Lack of participation in the group? Interview members to find out how they feel about the problem and about the issue's history. Talk to the teachers and staff who advise the group. Write an opinion defining the organization's problem and proposing one or more solutions.

6. Are you having a problem with your budget? Try keeping track of your expenditures and income, day by day, for a week. Categorize transactions—food, clothing, entertainment, and transportation, for example. Find unnecessary expenses or categories where you overspend frequently. Interview some of your friends to see how they handle their finances. Write an analysis of your budget problem and propose a solution for it.

7. Do you know someone who has a problem with a friendship or other relationship? Find some books or expert resources for advice on handling relationship problems. Write a brief definition of the problem as you see it. Make a list of solutions that sound workable to you.

Then, write an essay in which you put forth the problem and solutions, and hypothesize how the problem might be overcome.

More Challenging

8. Characters in fiction seldom consider all the alternatives for solving a problem. They often make decisions based on a limited perspective. Choose a character from a short story and analyze the problem he or she encounters. Offer possible solutions the character never considers. Conclude your analysis with a discussion of the most logical or beneficial resolution.

9. Scientists solve mysteries and find explanations by forming and testing hypotheses. After identifying a problem, they collect data and consult experts. Then, in order to identify patterns or trends in their information, scientists make comparisons and contrasts. Based on what they find, they decide on the most reasonable hypothesis and test their conclusions for acceptance, modification, or rejection. Choose a scientific concept or problem and follow the steps explained above. Write up the results of your experimentation as a problem-and-solution essay.

10. Suppose that you had to choose a new computer system for you and your classmates to use. What capabilities would you look for in the computer? Talk with a computer teacher to learn the desired features for classroom use. Look at several classroom computer systems and evaluate their costs, service contracts, and ease of use. Then, write a report in which you describe each system and present your opinion about which would be best for your classroom.

11. Your town has been plagued by the problem of pigeons nesting on building ledges and windowsills. The town council wants to install pigeon alarms—metal boxes that emit mock distress signals. These alarms work as decoys in reverse: The terrified cries of a petrified bird cause fellow pigeons to sense that there is a predator nearby. You're concerned with the moral problem of tricking and traumatizing the pigeons. In a letter to the town council, analyze both sides of the problem and suggest some alternate solutions.

Cooperative Activity

12. Do students object to the amount of time allowed for moving from one classroom to another? To the dress code? To an aspect of the physical environment at school, such as the lack of ventilation or light? Work with a partner to evaluate a problem at your school. One person should interview students about the problem; the other person should interview appropriate staff. Together, interview someone who is an expert concerning this kind of problem. Write a report presenting the problem and a reasonable solution to it. Include relevant quotes from each of the groups you interviewed.

Topic Bank for Chapter 12

Research: Research Paper

1. Choose a recent historical event about which you would like to know more. Read magazines and newspapers published at the time of the event. You might also contact historical societies or other organizations that have relevant information. In addition, try to interview people who were involved with or personally affected by the event. Use the results of your research to write a research paper.

2. Your computer literacy teacher wants you to do research on some aspect of computer technology. While he or she respects your ideas, you are not yet an expert. Therefore, concentrate on surveying, organizing, and objectively presenting all available facts and opinions on the topic of your choice. Begin by formulating a hypothesis about your topic that your research will lead you to accept, modify, or reject. For example, if you choose to write on the negative effects of computer games on children, you might hypothesize that while computer games increase hand-eye coordination, they interfere with creative problem-solving skills.

3. Cleopatra, Napoleon Bonaparte, Henry Ford, Mao Zedong—these are some of history's controversial figures, about whom diverse opinions have been expressed. Write a biographical report about someone many consider great, but who has also come under fire by some critics or historians. Evaluate the historical evidence to make your own case.

Less Challenging

4. At the movies these days, we are often dazzled by special effects—many of them computer-generated. While computers have provided incredible realism to modern special effects, the use of special effects can be traced back to the beginning of the motion picture industry. Using text, photos, and video, prepare a multimedia report on the history of special effects in motion pictures.

5. Choose a location in your town or neighborhood that you think may have an interesting past. Then, explore its history by researching old newspaper accounts, real-estate records, government documents, local history books, old photo albums, and any other sources you think may shed light on the history of the site. Interviews with senior citizens or members of a local historical society may also prove helpful. Chronicle your discoveries in a research paper.

6. The heyday of radio produced stars who, in their own way, were as well known and admired as the top movie actors. In fact, some stars appeared regularly in both movies and on the radio. Write a biographical report of a radio star such as Gracie Allen, Orson Welles, or Jack Benny. You may want to supplement your research paper with personal interviews of people who remember these stars' achievements.

7. In the 1930's, adults made dire predictions about what would happen to a generation of youth raised on swing music and the sounds of the Big Bands. Parents made similar complaints about Elvis Presley and the Beatles. Today, the forecasts of doom are made about teenagers who listen to heavy metal or rap. Write a research paper

describing the generation gap that music causes, as well as how the sounds of an era have affected its listeners.

More Challenging

8. In the 1940's, people read about laser technology mainly in science fiction. Since then, the technology has become an essential tool in many areas of our lives, including medicine and the space industry. Write a research paper on the history of laser technology or on some aspect of its present-day uses.

9. Ever since the Industrial Revolution changed the focus of advertising, both experts and the general public have debated the pros and cons of this field. Some psychiatrists have stated that advertising is permanently damaging to American society. Do you agree or disagree with this statement? How does advertising influence the beliefs and attitudes of people? Write a research paper in which you analyze both sides of this controversial topic. Use examples and facts to support your thesis.

10. Recently, you have been studying advanced technology and how it has changed scientific study. To extend your understanding, your science teacher has asked you to write a research paper debunking certain myths or old wives' tales (stories or warnings that persist in spite of evidence to the contrary). You might investigate such topics as the misconception that no two snowflakes are alike, the prohibition against swimming immediately after eating, or the illusion that all candy causes tooth decay. As you begin your research, interview experts and concentrate on finding the most recent scientific and medical data.

11. Try cultivating a plant you've never grown before, either from a seed package, a seed (or pit) found in the fruit of the plant, or a cutting from another plant. You might set up several pots under different conditions in order to offer recommendations on the best soil, lighting, fertilizer, and/or amount of water. Record the process and results, and write a lab report.

Cooperative Activity

12. In all walks of life, there are people who have interesting stories to tell about their work. With a group of your classmates, come up with a short list of people in different professions who might share some stories about their jobs—what education or training they needed, how they became interested in the profession, how they landed their first position, and what the work involves. As a group, compose a series of questions to ask the people who will be interviewed. Then, each person in the group should select one of the people to interview. Consider taking photographs or capturing the interview on audiotape or videotape. If possible, tape or photograph the people on the job. Finally, create a collection of biographical reports about the people and their work.

Topic Bank for Chapter 13

Response to Literature

1. Imagine that a national newsmagazine wants to promote the reading of fiction. They have decided to inaugurate a Story-of-the-Week feature. Which short story would get your nomination? Write a letter to the magazine editor in which you suggest a short story and explain why you are recommending it.

2. In his "A Celebration of Grandfathers," Rudolfo Anaya writes, "Remember the old people whose eyes seem like windows that peer into a distant past that makes absurdity of our contemporary world." (You can read this essay in *Prentice Hall Literature*, Gold.) Think of an old person you know who might fit this description—one whose eyes reveal knowledge or wisdom about the past. Write Anaya a letter telling him about that person. Then, ask Anaya for more information about his "old people." To whom is he referring? Ask any other questions you might have so that you can better compare the old person you know to Anaya's "old people."

3. Read "The Cask of Amontillado" by Edgar Allan Poe. (You can read this story in *Prentice Hall Literature*, Gold.) Respond to the story by writing a letter to Poe. By the end of the story, how do you feel about Montresor, the narrator? About Fortunato? Are you satisfied with the way the story ends? Tell Poe why you did or did not find the characters believable. Do you have a clear idea of why Montresor was planning to do a horrible thing to Fortunato? If not, advise Poe that he should give the reader more information in order to explain his character's motivation better.

4. Most detective stories, such as Arthur Conan Doyle's "The Redheaded League," contain elements of suspense. Read "The Redheaded League" or another detective story of your choosing. (You can read this story in *Prentice Hall Literature*, Gold.) Then, write a short paper in which you examine the aspects of the story that contribute to a feeling of mystery and suspense. Support your points with details from the story.

Less Challenging

5. Attend a movie or a play and write a review of it for your school newspaper. Begin by identifying the elements you can analyze, such as the acting, the setting, and the directing. Then, establish your criteria for evaluating each element. Be sure to gather specific evidence and details to support your judgments.

6. Poets attempt to convey a particular mood through the images in their poems. Read Marge Piercy's poem "To be of use," or another poem containing words that appeal to the senses. (You can read this poem in *Prentice Hall Literature*, Gold.) How does the poem make you feel? Does it remind you of any feelings you had in some previous experience? Which aspects of the poem are you particularly drawn to? Respond to these questions in a critical review. Use examples and quotations from the poem to support your opinion.

7. Many stories end with a surprising twist. Such a story is Guy de Maupassant's "The Necklace." Read "The Necklace," and then write

to Guy de Maupassant, telling him what you think of his story, particularly the ending. (You can read this story in *Prentice Hall Literature*, Gold.) Tell him what you did and did not like about the story. If you would prefer to see things work out differently for the main characters, suggest ways that Maupassant might change his story to make it more to your liking.

8. The message of a poem is often revealed through its images. Read "Memory" by Margaret Walker. (You can read this poem in *Prentice Hall Literature*, Gold.) Which images do you find especially effective or moving? What is the poet's message, and how do the images help the poet convey her message? Do you think the poet has made effective use of sound devices? Do they contribute to the message? Answer these questions and others that come to mind by writing a critical review of Walker's poem.

More Challenging

9. One of the pleasures of reading fiction is that we can often get closer to the characters than we can to people in real life. Short-story writers and novelists share with us the characters' innermost thoughts, feelings, and ideas. Choose a character that you feel particularly close to, and write an essay analyzing the techniques that the author uses to create this intimacy. In explaining what this fictional friend is like, consider both direct and indirect methods of characterization used by the author.

10. Suppose that you have been appointed to a committee to award a prize to the best nonfiction book written for high-school students during the past year. Choose a book about history, science, a famous person, or current affairs, and write an essay for the committee defending your choice. In addition to summarizing the content of the book, be sure to include your interpretation of the author's purpose and your evaluation of how he or she accomplishes it.

11. The meaning of James Thurber's short story "The Secret Life of Walter Mitty"—that a timid, insecure, and weak character can take refuge and find consolation in heroic fantasies—is fairly easy to grasp. (You can read this story in *Prentice Hall Literature*, Gold.) Write an essay in which you analyze the techniques that Thurber uses to convey this meaning. Begin by examining the repeated use of contrasts in moving back and forth between the "real" world of Walter Mitty and the more satisfying life of his daydreams. Notice, too, how the writer uses transitions and suggestive words and phrases to establish the links between Mitty's two worlds.

Cooperative Activity

12. As a group, brainstorm for a list of favorite poems. Identify the various themes and decide what, if anything, they have in common. Discuss the poems in terms of their imagery, figurative language, rhyme, and rhythm patterns. How do these poetic elements contribute to the meaning and mood of the poems? Each individual should write a literary analysis of one of the poems. Collect the finished analyses in a binder and create a table of contents and title for the collection of literary analyses.

Topic Bank for Chapter 14

Writing for Assessment

1. The transformation of a caterpillar into a butterfly is one of nature's wonders. Write an explanation of the process by which caterpillars become butterflies. Describe the transition step by step, describing the appearance of each form of the animal and identifying the seasons when each stage takes place.

2. Your class has been studying Latin American history for a few months and the subject is motivating all the students. Write a persuasive essay to a group of parents in an attempt to convince them that your class would benefit from a trip to Mexico during spring break. Use reason and maturity to formulate your arguments, describing the educational experiences that Mexico could offer.

3. Is there a right way and a wrong way to study for an exam? Use your personal experience to write an explanation of how to study for a mid-term exam. Tell your readers about surveying, questioning, reading, reciting, and reviewing their text. Discuss the advantages of forming study groups and quizzing one another.

4. Your principal is considering making uniforms part of the dress code. Write a persuasive letter to your school principal attempting to convince him or her to allow students to choose their own school dress rather than requiring uniforms. Be specific about what you would suggest as acceptable clothing for school wear. Describe the advantages of allowing students to wear street clothes instead of uniforms.

Less Challenging

5. A cousin your age, whom you have seen only a few times, is thinking about visiting you this summer. Write a letter to your cousin persuading him or her to come. Describe in colorful detail the members of your immediate family, as well as the social environment and the activities in which you both participate. Convey your enthusiasm for the visit and the fun you expect to have.

6. Do you know anyone who would make a good teacher? What qualities does that person possess? Write a persuasive essay about someone you think would make an excellent high-school teacher. Point out his or her personality characteristics that are important in a good teacher. Give specific examples about how this person might behave in different teaching situations.

7. Give a clear, logical explanation of how to prepare a simple dish, such as an omelette or spaghetti. List all the ingredients, and describe the process in step-by-step order, making sure to describe the textures and appearance of the dish.

8. For your school's annual Literary Conference, you have been asked to write a complimentary, persuasive essay about a book that you have read and enjoyed. Describe the characters, plot, and setting, using action words and adjectives that will help convince your audience to read the book.

More Challenging

9. Your positive experiences on the soccer team have motivated you to encourage other students to join so they can enjoy it, too. Write an essay to your classmates that will persuade them to try out for your soccer team in the spring. Give invigorating descriptions of the coach, the game, and the fans. Convince students who have never participated in sports before that they can excel at soccer and play as actively as their more-experienced teammates.

10. Some people who have never picked up a paintbrush may need some direction before starting a painting. Write step-by-step instructions to your classmates in art class on how to paint a watercolor. Be specific about the materials they will need and the techniques they will use. Encourage them to be uninhibited and impulsive in their style.

11. Write an explanation of the process of finding a summer job. Be specific about how to prepare a letter to a potential employer and how to dress for an interview. Prepare students to be honest and self-confident in their approaches. Discuss practical aspects of the job, such as schedule and salary.

12. You have committed an error on the job that cost the company a lot of money. The department supervisor is ready to fire you; however, company policy allows an employee to write a letter in his or her defense, offering reasons why he or she should not be let go. Write a letter to explain the circumstances for the error, express your regret, and offer reasons why you believe the mistake will never happen again.

Topic Bank for Chapter 15

Workplace Writing

1. Imagine that you have worked with a company for one year. Now, a new group of employees is about to start work at the company and your boss has asked you to prepare a welcoming speech for them. In your speech, sound friendly and enthusiastic. Explain why you think the new employees will like working there and offer them advice on how to succeed at their jobs. Warn them about any pitfalls they should watch out for. Make clear what they can expect from the company in exchange for their hard work and dedication.

2. Imagine that you are a supervisor at a company where employees are using their computers for playing games and browsing the Internet for personal enjoyment. Write a memo to all employees regarding this problem. In a friendly but firm tone, explain the company's policy on the matter. Tell what consequences employees will face if they continue to abuse their computer access. Also, explain any changes in company rules that you are initiating immediately.

3. You work at a firm that invents new products. In order to get a patent on an invention, however, you must show how the item differs from any similar type of product that preceded it. Fill out a patent application in which you first give the name of your invention and explain exactly what it does. Then, explain step by step how the invention works. Finally, detail how your invention is unique, explaining what makes it different from previous products.

Less Challenging

4. You are a bookkeeper in charge of financial records at a department store. Create a ledger that you can use to keep track of money that comes into and goes out of the store. Provide columns for sales, exchanges, and refunds, as well as one for miscellaneous expenditures. Enter some sample amounts to show how the ledger is used. Remember to leave an additional column to record the date of each entry in the ledger. Write a summary for your supervisor, explaining any unusual expenses or sales numbers.

5. Because of your computer expertise, your boss has asked you to design a Web site for your company. First, decide on the purpose of the Web site. Will it be to inform the public about your company's products and/or policies? Will it be to answer consumers' questions about your products and prices? Will the site have a different purpose altogether? Will it have many purposes? Write a proposal for your company's Web site that accomplishes the purposes you identify.

6. You have worked at the same position in a company for several years. Now, a promotion is available for one employee and you would like very much to fill the position. Fill out an application for the promotion. Begin by providing basic information, including your name, dates of employment in the company, and current position. Then, explain why you would like to receive the promotion. Tell why you feel you are best qualified for the job. Explain how your current job responsibilities have prepared you for the new position. Outline the special skills that you would be bringing to the job.

More Challenging

7. As director of development for a large corporation, you need to outline a five-year growth plan for the company. Explain how you plan to expand, cut back, or otherwise alter various departments over the coming years, including domestic and international sales, advertising, and research. For each change you propose, provide a clear, justifiable reason for it. Offer specific numbers and dollar amounts to show where you project the company will be in five years.

8. Imagine that you are the company supervisor for temporary employees who fill in for staff workers on a day-by-day basis. You must leave specific instructions for the temps, outlining the exact nature of their work. Write a different memo to each of three temporary workers. For each worker, explain his or her specific job and responsibilities. Be clear about when and where work should be delivered, and where office supplies can be found. Also, provide any other information about the office that you feel would be helpful.

9. You work in the Public Relations Department of a large manufacturer. You have received a letter from a concerned citizen who wants to know how your company is helping to safeguard the environment in the production and use of your product. Write a letter of reply to the concerned citizen. Explain the steps that your company has taken to comply with all government regulations regarding environmental protection. Show the person that there is no cause for concern regarding your product's environmental impact.

10. Imagine that you are a company employee who had to miss a week of work due to illness. In order not to lose any pay, you now need to fill out a company form that reports and explains your absence. Design and fill out a job absentee form. Give basic information about yourself, including your name, job title, and the dates of your absence. Give a detailed account of your illness, and provide the name of the doctor who attended to you. If you were in the hospital, supply the exact duration of your stay there.

Cooperative Activities

11. You and a few associates have just started your own company. You have about twenty employees and feel that certain office rules and policies need to be formulated. Working with a group, create a set of office guidelines for employees to follow. Each group member may focus on one particular area, such as dress code, social behavior, office neatness, or promptness. Each list should detail exactly what is expected of workers in that area. Collect all lists to create a company book of office guidelines.

12. You work for a company whose latest product has proven to be a complete failure. Rather than eliminate it, the company president has appointed a special team to reevaluate the product, research the reasons for its failure, and devise a strategy to reintroduce it. Working with a group, decide exactly how you would re-release the product to the public. Each group member should be in charge of a different department, such as design, advertising, marketing, and pricing. Each group member should explain why the product failed initially, as it relates to his or her area, and then explain why the new campaign will be more successful.